PUZZLE JOURNEY INTO SPACE

Story devised by Rebecca Heddle

Written by Lesley Sims

Illustrated by Annabel Spenceley

Designed by Lucy Smith

Space consultant: Martin Lunn

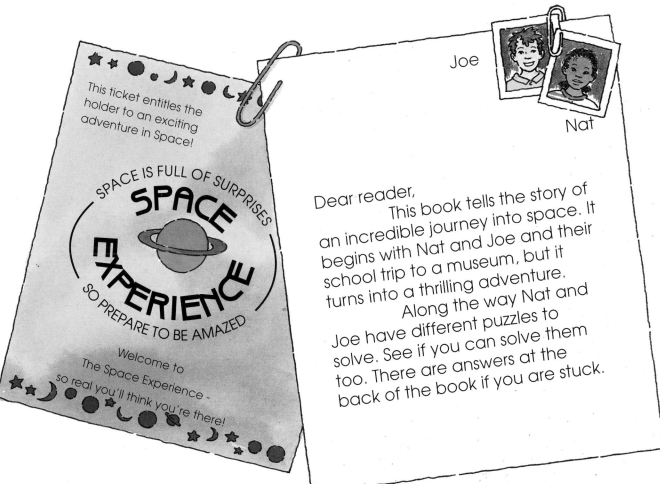

This ticket entitles the holder to an exciting adventure in Space!

SPACE IS FULL OF SURPRISES

SPACE EXPERIENCE

SO PREPARE TO BE AMAZED

Welcome to
The Space Experience -
so real you'll think you're there!

Joe

Nat

Dear reader,
        This book tells the story of an incredible journey into space. It begins with Nat and Joe and their school trip to a museum, but it turns into a thrilling adventure.
        Along the way Nat and Joe have different puzzles to solve. See if you can solve them too. There are answers at the back of the book if you are stuck.

Series Editor: Gaby Waters

A new spaceship

Nat and Joe were on a school trip to the Space Experience, the biggest space museum in the world.

As they waited to go in, Nat grew more and more excited. "I want to be an astronaut," she said.

Joe grunted. He wasn't interested in space and he didn't like museums. "I'd rather be playing football," he muttered.

When they got inside at last, they saw a spacesuit and shiny models of rockets and satellites on display.

There were huge pictures of planets and far-off galaxies covering the walls. But Joe was bored.

Models and pictures weren't much fun. Then he felt Nat tugging the back of his t-shirt.

"Follow me!" she said. "I've found something much more exciting."

She dragged Joe along a corridor lined with photographs and posters.

"This doesn't look any more interesting to me," he grumbled.

It's just a big plane!

But the corridor led into an enormous hall which was almost filled by a plane.

"Look!" said Nat. "It's a model of the very latest space shuttle!"

She dashed inside. "What are you doing?" said Joe and followed her.

Nat sat down in front of a screen and eagerly hit a few buttons. Suddenly the doors slid shut.

In a panic Joe tried to open them. Nat didn't even notice. She was too busy playing astronauts.

What's happening?

"Three... two... one... Lift off!" said Nat as a joke. But the cockpit filled with a loud roaring noise.

Into space

Joe quickly sat down beside Nat and they stared out of the window. They could see the whole Earth in it and it was growing smaller and smaller.

"This model spaceship is great!" said Joe. "It really feels as if we've taken off."

Look at the Earth!

IT'S ONLY A TOOL LEFT BEHIND BY SOME CARELESS ASTRONAUT. THERE ARE MORE THAN 7,000 PIECES OF JUNK UP HERE.

Nat was amazed too. But before she could reply, an object drifted across a screen in front of them.

"What's that?" asked Nat. As she spoke a message appeared on the screen with the answer.

"Do you think the ship can hear us?" she asked Joe in surprise. Joe wasn't listening. He was staring at the screen again.

Now it showed the moon, growing bigger and bigger. Then it appeared in the window, dusty grey and covered with craters.

Seconds later, they felt a gentle thud. The noise from the engines stopped.

"It's incredible!" cried Joe. "It's just as if we've landed on the moon."

4

"Let's see what it's like outside," said Nat. "We'll need spacesuits." She jumped up and began searching through all the drawers in the cabin.

Joe was doubtful. "We're still in the museum," he said. "Outside it's just that big hall."

But Nat had found two large white suits and some jumbo-sized gloves.

"I wonder what it's like to walk on the moon," she said, struggling into the strange space underwear.

"We'll never know," said Joe's muffled voice, from under his bulky jacket. Nat ignored him.

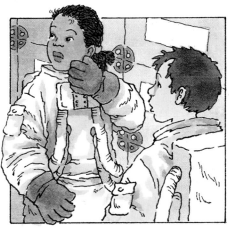

"Now where are the helmets?" she wondered.

Do you know?

5

Walking on the moon

Just wearing the suits made them feel excited as they left the cabin. It seemed to take ages for the outer door to open. When it finally slid back they stared out in astonishment, hardly believing their eyes.

"Wow! It really looks like the moon!" said Nat, as she climbed down the ladder.

"It's weird, I feel so light!" said Joe delightedly, as he jumped off the bottom rung.

Nat followed more slowly. The big suit and boots were hard to move in, although they weren't heavy. Joe was jumping around as if his boots had springs on.

On the last rung Nat paused. Here goes! she thought and stepped off the ladder.

Joe grinned and said something but Nat couldn't hear a word he was saying.

Why was he mouthing words at her? Nat wondered. He looked like an excited goldfish.

Then she remembered. In space, astronauts used radios in their suits to talk to each other.

Joe jogged up to a large boulder and kicked it. "It's a goal!" he cried as the rock bounced away.

"These rocks are as light as beach balls," Joe said, lifting one above his head. "Hey Nat, catch!"

Nat looked up to see a huge rock flying straight at her. She hit it back gently and it soared past Joe.

Look! They've used wire to make the flag stick out.

It flew over his head and landed near a flag of stars and stripes.

"This was left by the first men on the moon," said Nat. "Their footprints are still here! There's no wind or rain to wash them away."

She looked at the ground. "That's odd!" she said.

What has Nat noticed?

7

Men on the moon?

Joe and Nat were carried inside and left in front of a large screen. They were terrified. What was going on?

Suddenly a picture appeared. To their surprise it showed a man sitting behind a large control panel, in a room full of machines.

"Have you stolen a spaceship?" asked the man on the screen. "Oh dear." He made the two words sound like a threat.

He scowled at Nat and Joe, as if he could see them through the screen. "Did you think the moon was deserted?" he asked.

Joe was puzzled. He was sure he'd seen the man's face before, but where?

Do you know?

Escape

The man stood up. His image towered over them.

Nat struggled but her robot didn't let go. Then Joe covered the light on his robot and they fell.

As Joe got up, something on the floor caught his eye.

Joe picked it up and raced after Nat to the door. But the robots were close behind.

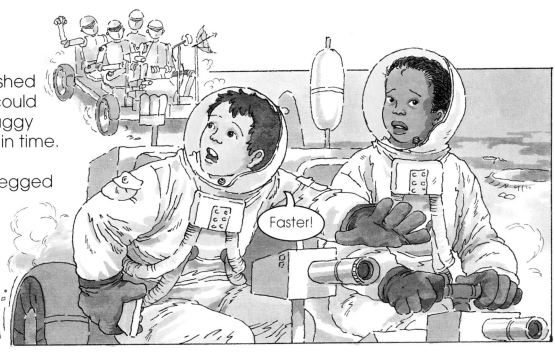

Nat frantically pushed every button she could see. Finally the buggy started – only just in time.

"Hurry up!" Joe begged looking behind them.

A buggy full of robots was hot on their trail and catching up fast.

As they reached the ship, Nat cried out in despair. More robots were already guarding it.

With robots in front and behind, they were trapped. How would they ever escape?

Joe looked at the remote control he'd found. "I think we can give the robots orders with this," he said. "But I don't know which buttons to press."

In a flash, Nat thought of something she'd seen in the angry man's office. "I know the ones we need," she said in relief.

Do you?

Computer speak

Joe and Nat ran into the ship. The doors closed, the engines roared and a strange voice said, "Hi!"

Wh - Who said that?

Then a shiny green head appeared on the screen. "I'm K67389, Phase 3 Deluxe, your computer," it said. "Call me K." The head grinned. "Ready for adventure, moon rovers?" it asked. But its smile soon vanished.

"Oh no!" it said. "Asteroids!" Nat and Joe looked out of the window in terror. Huge lumps of rock were hurtling past.

"I'll put a heat map on screen and you plot a safe route. Avoid the blue rocks – they're asteroids," said K the computer.

Can you find a way through?

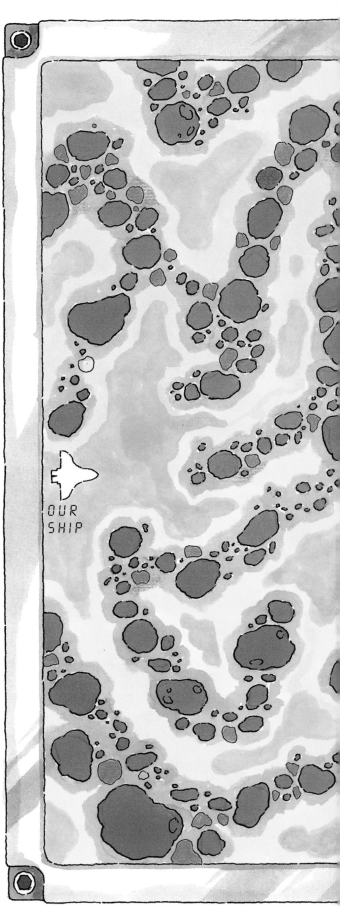

OUR SHIP

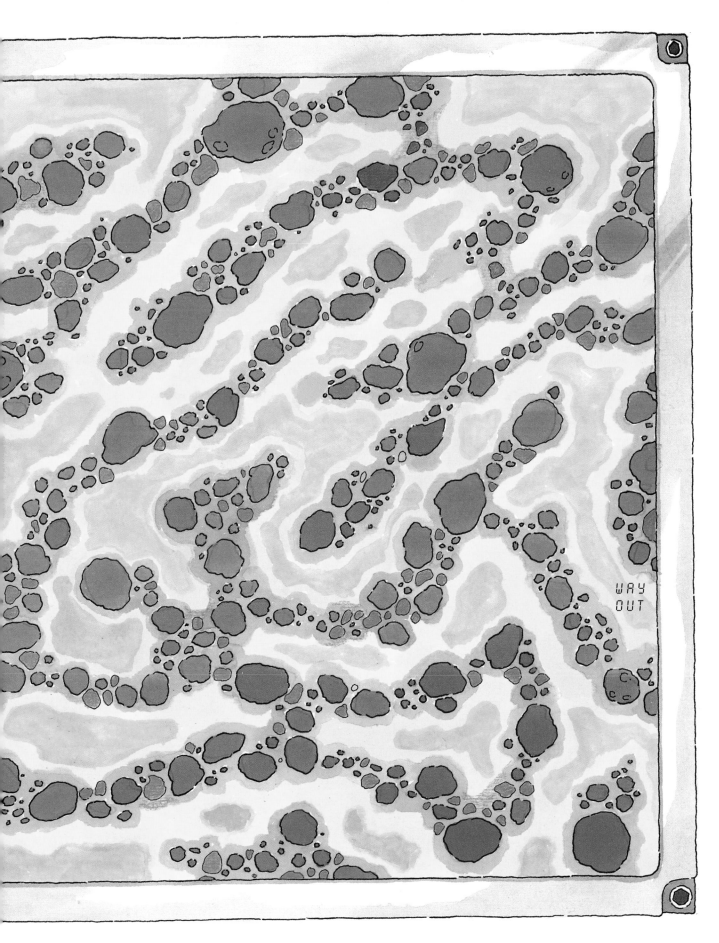

WAY
OUT

A gas giant

The ship swung from side to side to avoid the asteroids. Nat and Joe were flung all over the deck.

At last the ship was safely through and flying deeper into space.

A planet loomed up in the window. "That's Jupiter," K told them. "It's big. A thousand times bigger than Earth. But it's mostly made of gas so we can't land on it."

Nat and Joe stared at Jupiter as it came closer. A giant red spot was spinning on the surface.

"That's some storm," said K. "It's been whirling for hundreds of years."

After the bumpy ride through the asteroids, Nat's head was spinning and whirling too.

"I feel sick," she moaned. She staggered back and her elbow accidentally hit a large red button.

Suddenly the ship was thrown on its side, right in the path of an empty spaceship.

14

"Hang on!" said K, swerving around it. "That was a probe going to Pluto. It won't stop for anything. But we could stop. How about a planet prowl?"

K's head grew big on the screen. "Where shall we land?" he asked. "If I show you a space chart, you can decide."

Is there anywhere we can't land?

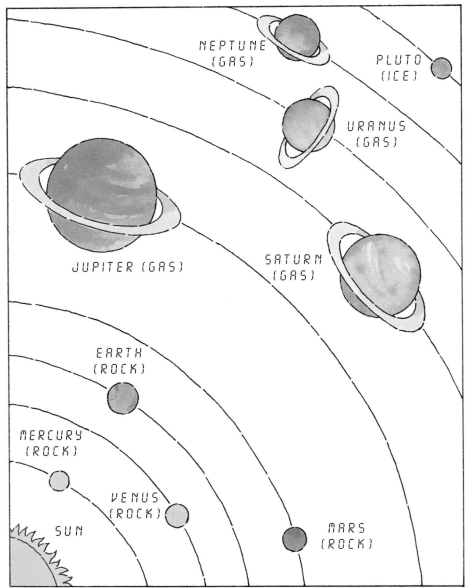

NEPTUNE (GAS)

PLUTO (ICE)

URANUS (GAS)

JUPITER (GAS)

SATURN (GAS)

EARTH (ROCK)

MERCURY (ROCK)

VENUS (ROCK)

MARS (ROCK)

SUN

We can't fly any deeper into space or we won't have fuel to get home. And we can't go closer to the sun than Earth. It's too hot.

Joe and Nat studied the chart. They soon realized that there was only one planet they could land on, apart from Earth.

Which planet is it?

Comet clash

"Mars!" said Nat excitedly, flicking through a book on planets. She read it out to Joe.

Joe didn't hear. He was looking for food. Nat was too excited to eat but space travel had made Joe hungry.

It's half the size of Earth. No one has ever walked on it before . . .

He found several drawers crammed with packets of dried food.

He would have preferred a burger but he heated some anyway.

He ate the food out of the packets. It was very sticky but it tasted really good.

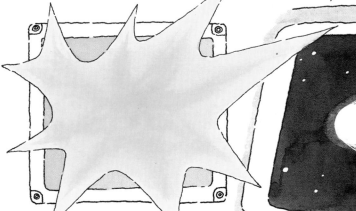

Suddenly, a bright flash filled one screen. "What's that?" said Joe, nearly dropping his tray.

"I think it's a comet going past!" cried Nat. She ran to the window to watch as it shot by.

The comet's tail streamed out behind it, a haze of shimmering stardust and fragments of rock.

Then BANG! The whole ship rocked and Nat and Joe were thrown back.

"Did we hit something, K?" asked Joe in a panic. But there was no answer.

Instead a message appeared on one of the screens.

I CAN'T SEE WHAT'S AHEAD. SOMETHING IN THE VIEWER MUST BE BROKEN. WE'LL HAVE TO STOP UNTIL WE FIND OUT WHAT IT IS AND FIX IT. I'LL TEST COMPUTER COMPONENTS. YOU CHECK THE REST.

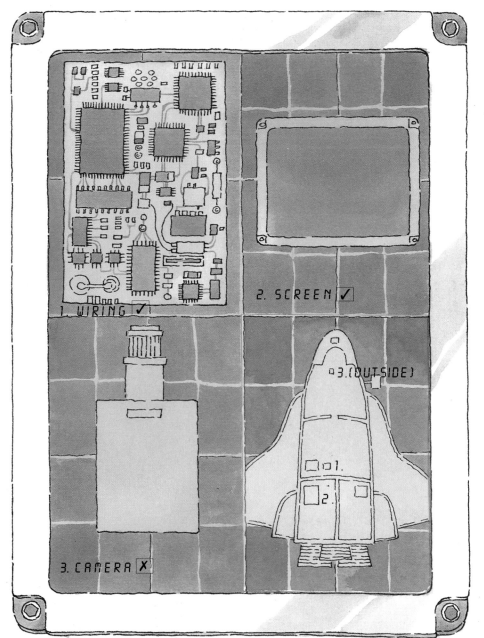

1. WIRING ✓

2. SCREEN ✓

3. [OUTSIDE]

1.

2.

3. CAMERA ✗

Where do we start?

Nat and Joe began to look around, but they didn't really know what they were looking for.

The engines stopped and the ship grew quiet. Soon the only sound was a faint hum from K.

Nat looked at the control panel. One of the screens was covered with fuzzy lines. A moment later four pictures came up on another screen.

It was very clear which part was broken. They could even see where on the ship they would find it.

What needs mending?

Stepping outside

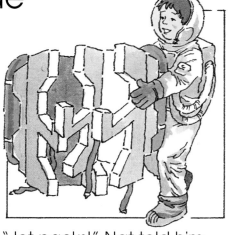

Nat and Joe quickly put on their suits. "How do we move outside?" said Joe.

"Jet packs!" Nat told him pointing to a locker. Joe carried them over.

"These are like armchairs!" he said, leading the way outside.

It seems to go on forever.

It's an awfully long way home.

The outer door opened, leaving Nat and Joe gazing out onto a million miles of blackness. For a second, it felt like they were the only two people in the universe.

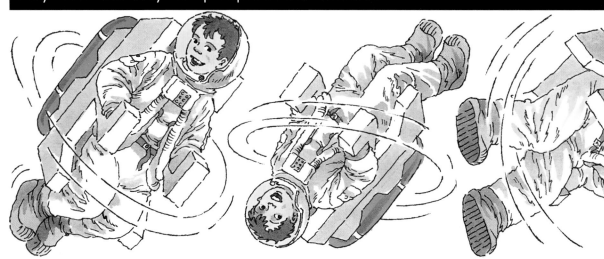

Then Joe switched his jet pack on. "This is fun!" he yelled going one way.

"Better than football!" he shouted, going the other way.

"Try looping the loop!" he called to Nat from upside down.

Eventually they remembered why they had gone outside and started to look for the camera.

"It's down there," Joe said, pointing to the roof of the shuttle. "But it doesn't look broken to me."

They flew closer to investigate.

It must have been hit by some of that comet dust.

"The lens is broken and there's a hole in the panel on this side," Nat said as she put the tool box down.

Oops!

Joe tried to unscrew the panel. But pushing on the screwdriver pushed him away from the ship.

Nat had to hold him in place, keeping herself still by holding a handle on the side of the ship.

As Joe took the panel off, he accidentally dropped one of the screws. It hung in space before him. "Amazing!" he said.

Nat sorted through all the new parts in the tool box. "I hope everything's here," she said.
Can you find what they need?

Off to Mars

With the camera mended they flew on. The ship sped through space, but the journey to Mars still took a couple of hours.

As they neared the planet, one of the screens began to flash.

SOMETHING HAS GONE WRONG WITH THE AUTO PILOT. YOU'LL HAVE TO LAND THE SHIP. SWITCHING TO MANUAL NOW!

It was an urgent message from K. Joe watched in horror as Nat took control.

She grabbed the joystick, shut her eyes and pushed. The ship bumped to a halt.

Joe looked out in relief. "Hey, the sky's red! I bet it's hot out there," he said.

IT'S COMING FROM A DRY CHANNEL NOT FAR FROM THE SHIP, BETWEEN THREE POINTED ROCKS, A SQUARE ROCK AND A CRATER.

"No, you galaxy gazer, it's cold," said K as they put on their suits. "But there is a warm spot. How odd."

Nat and Joe hovered in the doorway as K told them what to look for, to find the warm spot.

Leaving the ship, Nat paused. "We'll be the first humans to walk on Mars. Anything could happen!"

They felt much heavier than they had on the moon. A wind blew dusty red sand all around them. Keeping together, they tried to look for the landmarks K had listed.

"Mars is covered in craters and rocks," Joe sighed. "We'll be here forever." But Nat thought she'd found the right place.

Can you see where they should go?

Into the planet

There was a tunnel leading down from the channel.

Should we go down?

If we don't, we'll always wonder what was there.

It's large enough to squeeze through.

Joe carefully lowered himself into the tunnel.

Nat stayed close behind.

Don't go without me!

They felt their way along a dark passageway.

I can't see a thing.

Me neither. Ow! Watch where you're going.

You are who?

From you are where?

Wait! I just heard something!

Me too. Was it like a voice in your head?

The voice stopped and a brilliant yellow light clicked on.

The light was so bright it hurt even through their tinted helmets.

Aliens from come you have where? Mars to welcome!

As their eyes grew used to the light, they looked around. They were surrounded by live rocks! Then the voice spoke again. It was talking backwards.

Did it call us aliens? We're not aliens!

Ssh! Er, hello! We come from Earth.

Front to back speak they where planet green blue the yes ah!

To their amazement Joe and Nat realized it was a rock they could hear in their heads! It spoke again and they saw pictures of its thoughts too.

All at talk didn't and hard and cold were they but flew they. Before Earth from visitors had we've.

Brains alien's the you are? Out came you when surprised were we. Them inside you like anything have didn't they.

Um, not exactly.

Landing bumpy very a had you. watch to stayed we so arrived you when surface the on up were we.

"We didn't see anyone when we landed," said Joe. "Where were you?"

Look back at page 21. How many rock people can you see?

The Martian caves

"Wow!" said Joe. "This is incredible. I can hardly believe it. Talking rocks!"

The voice in his head grew cross. "Rocks eat we. Martians we're rocks not we're. ROCKS?! Rocks?"

"Sorry," mumbled Joe.

A different voice entered their minds. "Way this! Mars of tour a like you'd perhaps?"

Nat and Joe followed the Martian down stone steps and into a large cave. It was full of sleeping, grunting rocks. They tiptoed through.

In the next cave, Martians were chipping rocks from the walls. Their guide picked up a chunk to chew.

"They must have iron teeth!" Joe whispered.

They climbed down to the third cave. One Martian was weaving cloth on a large stone frame. Another was leaning over a stone sink mixing paint and splashing it everywhere.

Make to years two takes blanket each.

Rocks crushed from made is paint the.

Music rock!

In the fourth cave they arrived in the middle of a concert.

Suddenly the music stopped. Their guide looked surprised.

"Visitor another?!" he said. "Alien flying another seen has scouts our of one."

To Nat and Joe's alarm, a picture of a spaceship appeared in their minds.

Why are they worried?

A new arrival

Nat and Joe hurried to the surface.

We must go and guard our ship.

You wait here. We don't think the pilot is very friendly.

But above ground they ran straight into a waiting robot.

Leave us alone!

Why have you come here?

Why are you chasing us? What do you want?

It's your spaceship. I've never seen one like it!

I didn't mean to frighten you. I just haven't spoken to anyone for so long . . .

I've been following you since you left the moon. My ship's so old, it's taken me all this time to get here.

If I could build a ship like yours, I could explore the galaxy.

I'm fed-up with the moon. I've been stuck there for twenty years with only robots for company.

How were you stuck on the moon?

Nat and Joe listened, amazed, as the astronaut told his story.

I always wanted to be an astronaut. Finally I flew to the moon.

I was stuck on board at first. But later, I stayed on the moon as part of an experiment.

Then disaster! Before I could fly back to Earth, my ship exploded.

I was stranded. For a while I didn't mind. I was sure someone would rescue me in the end. But no one came.

So I built a base using things other astronauts had left behind. Then I built robots for company. I even built two rockets. But I didn't know if they would fly, so I launched the first one empty.

Finally I made a satellite dish to beam messages to other life forms. But nobody replied. I'm a scientist and explorer. I need new challenges. I need new places to explore.

Mars explore could you.

As he finished, five Martians appeared. The astronaut looked shocked. "Have I gone crazy? I can hear voices in my head!" he said.

You do?

It to happened what know don't we but moon the from off take made you rocket first the saw we. Us it's crazy not you're!

Heading for home

"The ship I made reached Earth?" said the astronaut when Nat told him. He could hardly believe it. "What's so funny?" he asked, as Martians began to stream out from under the ground, all rolling around with laughter.

A Martian grinned. "One were you thought planet your on people the and aliens see to wanted you!"

The astronaut smiled too. "Keep your ship!" he said to Nat and Joe. "I can't wait to explore Mars."

"You'd better hurry home before someone notices you've gone and a brand new spaceship is missing."

Within minutes they were back on board and out of their spacesuits.

"You won't believe it, K," cried Nat. "We found aliens on Mars!"

"I think you've been in space too long," K said.

Down to earth

"Seat belts on, you alien spotters!" K said firmly as the engines roared to zoom them back to Earth.

"Nearly home!" K added as Earth appeared on the screen, growing bigger and bigger . . .

The next thing they knew the ship's door opened and a man was helping them out.

Feeling puzzled they went in search of their class. "It's as if we never took off," said Joe, putting his hands in his pockets. They felt very full.

Curiously he emptied everything onto a table. There it was, proof they really had been to space.

Which things did they bring back from space? Look back through the book to see where they found them.

29

Facts about space

Nat and Joe spent the rest of the day in the Space Experience. They found out lots of facts about the places they had visited. Later they made a display for their classroom wall.

There is no weather on the moon, so the footprints left by astronauts will be there for ten million years.

The moon takes the same time to turn around as it does to go around the Earth. This means that one side is always facing away from the Earth.

The first men landed on the moon in 1969 and the last ones in 1972. They left over 50000kg (110230lb) of litter.

Comets are made of ice and dust. Some scientists call them dirty snowballs. As a comet comes close to the sun, the sun's heat melts some of the ice. This forms the comet's tail.

Asteroids are rocks which circle the sun between Mars and Jupiter. Some are small but the biggest is about the size of France.

The moon only has one-sixth of Earth's gravity. Everything feels a sixth as heavy on the moon as it does on Earth.

The rings around Saturn and Uranus are made of millions of chunks of ice and can be seen from Earth.

Only three space craft have ever been as far out in the solar system as Saturn. The last one, Voyager 2, took four years to reach Saturn. It went on to visit Uranus and Neptune.

by Nat and Joe

Answers to puzzles

pages 4-5 Into space

The helmets are in a locker behind Nat. It is circled in this picture.

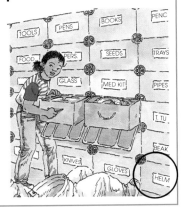

pages 6-7 Walking on the moon

Nat has noticed these extra footprints. Some of them cover the astronauts' footprints so they are newer, but they are different from Nat and Joe's.

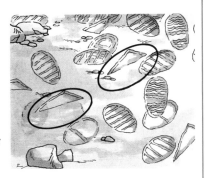

pages 8-9 Men on the moon?

Joe saw the man before on this poster in the Space Experience.

pages 10-11 Escape

Joe can make the robots go back to their base by pressing the combination 317*. Nat remembers seeing it on a piece of paper on the astronaut's desk in the base.

pages 12-13 Computer speak

The way through the asteroids is shown in black.

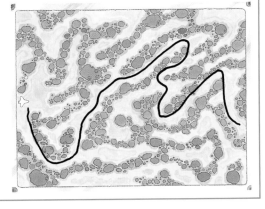

pages 14-15 A gas giant

The only planet Joe and Nat can land on is Mars. The gas planets have no solid surface and all the others apart from Earth are too far away or too close to the sun.

pages 16-17 Comet clash

The camera is the part which is broken. The fourth picture shows that it is outside the ship.

pages 18-19 Stepping outside

The parts they need are circled below.

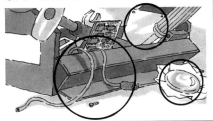

pages 20-21 Off to Mars

The landmarks are circled below. The warm spot is marked with an X.

pages 22-23
Into the planet

There are nine rock people on page 21. They are circled in this picture.

pages 24-25
The Martian caves

Nat and Joe are worried that the astronaut from the moon is landing on Mars. They saw this picture of the rocket in his base on the moon.

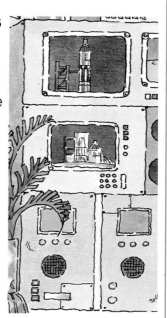

pages 26-27
A new arrival

The ship reached Earth. There was a picture of it on display at the Space Experience on page 2. It is under the label "Alien ship?"

Alien ship?

Ryan Rocket | Landed on Earth 1995

page 29 Down to Earth

These are the things Joe brought back from space.

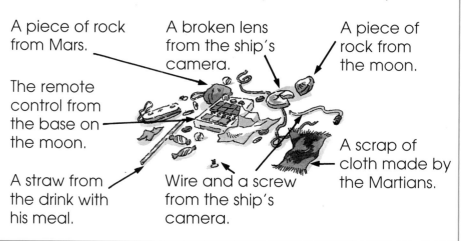

A piece of rock from Mars.

A broken lens from the ship's camera.

A piece of rock from the moon.

The remote control from the base on the moon.

A scrap of cloth made by the Martians.

A straw from the drink with his meal.

Wire and a screw from the ship's camera.

This edition first published in 2003 by Usborne Publishing Ltd., Usborne House, 83-85 Saffron Hill, London EC1N 8RT, England.

www.usborne.com Copyright © 2003, 1995 Usborne Publishing Ltd.

U.E. Printed in Portugal.

First published in America March 1996.